+|'me'S-pace

bk. 1
vol. 2

"For Love Alone"
Christina'S-tead

An examination of the
English Tongue
from the viewpoint of
poetry

doc. 001b
society for cUm|n' linguistics
(scUm)

compiled by
chr|st|ne werthe|m

with an Introduction by
Dodie Bellamy

TRENCHART: The Casements Series

$\oint$

LES FIGUES PRESS
Los Angeles

Designed and edited by Les Figues Press.
Visual art by Lisa Darms
Printed in Canada.

FIRST EDITION

ISBN 10: 0-9766371-9-7
ISBN 13: 978-0-9766371-9-6
Library of Congress Control Number: 2007900857

The TRENCHART Casements series is made possible through the contributions of the Les Figues Press membership. Les Figues Press thanks these members for their support and encouragement.

Les Figues Press would like to acknowledge the following individuals for their generosity: David Arata, Tracy Bachman, Nancy Bauer-King, Peter Binkow, Johanna Blakley, Diane & Chris Calkins, Kate Chandler, Sarah de Heras, Deborah Harrington, Jennifer Mayer, Susan McCabe, Carolyn K. Place, Vanessa Place, Stanley Sheinbaum, Mary & Jim Swanson, Julie Wilhoit and Heather Wilson.

TRENCHART is a project of Les Figues Press, a nonprofit 501(c)3 publisher of unconventional literary prose and poetics. TRENCHART titles are available in select independent bookstores and online at www.spdbooks.com. Becoming a member is the best way to ensure your complete collection of TRENCHART titles. For membership information, see the Press website at: www.lesfigues.com.

Publisher's Note: Special thanks to Johanna Blakley, Janet Sarbanes, Sarah Simons, Matias Viegener, Maude Place and Fergus Place.

Distributed by SPD / Small Press Distribution
1341 Seventh Street
Berkeley, CA 94710
www.spdbooks.org

TrenchArt 2/3
Book 4 of 5 in the TRENCHART Casements Series.

LES FIGUES PRESS
PO Box 35628
Los Angeles, CA 90035
323.934.5898 / info@lesfigues.com
www.lesfigues.com

+o

|'me

what shivers
between the ₚᵣₒ position of |
+ ₁'ₘ position of me / O
+ +|'me + +|'me + +|'me + +|'me +
|'me |'me |'me |'me
O | O | O |
Oooooooh
|'me.

Contents

The Slit

an introduction

Mother, you are the one mouth / I would be a tongue to.

Sylvia Plath, "Poem for a Birthday"

In 7th grade math I received a F in conduct for encouraging my classmates to repeat the tongue twister: How many sheep could the sheep slitter slit when the sheep slitter was out slitting sheep? Our tongues would slip around our mouths uncontrollably and we'd spit out "shitting sheep." Averting our gazes from the chalky algebraic scrawls on the blackboard, we'd cover our mouths, hunch in our desks and guffaw. Researching tongue twisters online I find that it's supposed to be sheet slitter, not sheep slitter. Paper or perhaps bed sheets being slit as opposed to my horrific vision of a field of eviscerated sheep. Reading +|'me'S-pace reminded me of this story, for both point to the brute violence beneath the language game.

+|'me'S-pace describes itself as a work of litteral poetics, i.e., a method for studying psychic structure in the English tongue. Why the extra "t" in litteral? Litter as in a bed as in debris as in an accumulation over time, littoral as in seashore, as in the Latin *littera*, "letter." On dictionary.com I read: "Literally is often used erroneously, even by writers like Dryden and Pope, to indicate 'what follows must be taken in the strongest admissible sense' (1687), which is opposite to the word's real meaning," real as in the Latin *litteralis* "of or belonging to letters or writing." Litteral poetics experiments in "worders," a small tweak to wonders. In its ecstatic exploration of the "English tongue" it never forgets the body, the English tongue no longer an abstraction but an organ of perception. Language collapses into shivers and sighs, the body-mouth convulsing with puns, allusions, potty humor. Punctuation moistens a text that simultaneously clings and negates, clings and negates, a text that pulses with waves of meaning, waves of being.

In litteral poetics authorship/self is not singular but a society. +|'me'S-pace is document 001b of the society for cUm|n' linguistics (scUm). scUm harkens back to the violent upheavals of

Valerie Solanas' 1967-8 manifesto. I fixate on that cUm, stare at it until the letters float in the air and rearrange themselves before my eyes, as did Tom Hanks in *The Da Vinci Code* movie. U c m. You see m. Throughout the text "m" is associated with me, with mothers, with the rhythm of time. You see me. As Tom Hanks would say, "A clue?" Back to the original sequence: cUm: see You Me: you and me relinquish their subject/object (op)positions, form a utopia in which You and Me are linked, are naughty-naughty in bed together, always cUm|n'/cumming. cUm as in "together with," as in *magna cum laude*, as in "slumber party-cum-bloodbath" (the bizarre example www.dictionary.com uses to define "cum").

Christine Wertheim cum Christina 'S-tead. *"For Love Alone"*_{Christina'S-tead} the uber-text of +|'me'S-pace, shares its title with the 1944 novel by the late Australian modernist Christina Stead. The 1944 *For Love Alone* begins:

> In the part of the world Teresa came from, winter is in July, spring brides marry in September, and Christmas is consummated with roast beef, suckling pig, and brandy-laced plum pudding at 100 degrees in the shade, near the tall pine-tree loaded with gifts and tinsel as in the old country, and old carols have rung out all through the night.

Both projects celebrate a poetics of the topsy-turvy. No matter how hard we try to ignore the for-granted, it stands out stark and alien as a surrealist sculpture.

At first glance, +|'me'S-pace frightened me. I looked at all the weird typography and symbols and thought I'm too stupid for this, I don't have the patience, I'll never get it, all those slashes and plusses and apostrophes, it looks so abstract I don't want to go there. I could not have been more wrong. In this text the sheep slitter is everywhere. Look at those pervasive slashes. The slash is I the slash is it. The slash divides yet connects. It carves out new syllables, new rhythms, new linguistic masses. It fills a space yet creates a gap. Infusing the poetic text with non-Roman alphabet notation subverts rote readings, rote reactions. To take it in, you have to read backwards and forward, sometimes upside-down. Letters disappear

and appear in waves. Words break apart and reform—
something's added, something's missing.

The rhythm of +|'me'S-pace is not the monotone
drone of alpha but the visionary zeal of low theta
where connections run rampant. The text mutates and
writhes across the space-time continuum in a dance of
Burroughsian excess where linguistic mishaps predict
the future. Suddenly you're on the dancefloor with it,
in sync, feeling the pulse. Above your head a disco ball
slits the light, refracting rainbows. I read +|'me'S-pace on
New Year's Eve and it thrust me into such an altered
state I couldn't talk, so I went to a DJ-ed party and
danced my brains out. My friends danced around me,
their wide smiles felt slow motion, too loud to even
shout, our bodies flapping like tongues. Not alone,
gyrating *For Love Alone*. Thump thump thump.

Let language come alive. Let its characters
collide and caress, enacting an ancient, primal drama
of desire, separation anxiety, domination and sex. Sex
is everywhere as is its shadow, the terror of the void.
Let fluid meanings multiply out of our control like
rabbits. Meanings sneak up on us that are impossible
to articulate. All these maddeningly multiple meanings
and connections subvert the atomism built into the
system, opening the possibility of hope. Litteral
poetics embodies the multiplicity called for by the
French feminists without limiting it to a female thing:
I have multiple orgasms and therefore I need to subvert
logocentricity and write in this new messy female way.
+|'me'S-pace is far from messy and refreshingly unstupid.

As +|'me'S-pace points out over and over again,
those of us infected with the English tongue inhabit
a realm which privileges sons and mothers, in which
there is no room, no structure for daughters and fathers.
In my memory the tongue twister goes: Where was
the sheep slitter's daughter while the sheep slitter was
out slitting sheep. I know this is a false memory, an
alternate realm in which it's fathers and daughters the
tongue slips over. That mysterious daughter—where
is she, what slippery clever things is she doing behind
her father's back? She's thriving in LA and she's
writing books like +|'me'S-pace.

Dodie Bellamy

San Francisco, 2007

+|'me'S-pace

doc. 001b
society for cUm|n' linguistics
(scUm)

compiled by
chr|st|ne werthe|m

Litteral Poetics

An Introduction to the scUm Methodology

> For the same Seeds compose both Earth and Seas,
> The Sun, and Moon, Fruits, Animals, and Trees,
> But their contexture, or their motion disagrees.
> So in my Verse are Letters common found
> To many words unlike in sense and sound;
> Such great variety bare change affords
> Of order in th' few Elements of Words.
>
> And hence, as We discours'd before, we find
> It matters much with what first Seeds we joyn'd,
> Or how, or what position they maintain,
> What motion give, and what receive again:
> And that the Seeds remaining still the same,
> Their order chang'd, of wood are turn'd to flame.
> Just as the letters little change affords
> Ignis and Lignum, two quite different words.

Lucretius, De Rarum Natura

The tradition of litteral poetics covers an extraordinary range of writing projects, many of which are rarely found today in either literary compendiums or in works of linguistic scholarship. For instance, it includes the nineteenth century soldier-turned-linguist, Jean-Pierre Brisset, who deduced by etymological research that man is descended from frog, (see *Imagining Language* by J. Rasula and S. McCaffery). It also includes the Roman poet and philosopher Titus Lucretius Carus whom many contemporary writers regard as an experimentalist *avant la lettre* and for whom, not just The Word, but *all* words are to be taken literally.

For example, in Latin, the tongue in which Lucretius toiled, the word for fire, *Ignis,* is a partial anagram of *Lignum,* the word for wood. This extraordinary fact told Lucretius that, just as Democritus believed the variety of matter could be explained as different arrangements of a group of material atoms, so the variety of words could be explained as the different arrangements of a set of atomic characters.

Many nineteenth century thinkers, from William Rowan Hamilton to Freud's mentor, Brentano, also believed that arrangements found in nature and mathematics were manifest in language, and more importantly, in the *shifts* from one set of meanings to another. Indeed, this is the idea at the heart of Freud's free association method for analyzing unconscious structures. And much contemporary combinatorial writing that composes itself by accumulating vast banks of material through following the associations of a small set of randomly chosen source terms (words, places, times, events, people, etc.) works by a similar process, though this is the exact inverse of Freud's method, where the purpose is to distill the small random source set from the masses accreted around it.

The idea at the heart of all these methods is what the philosopher of language Jean-Jacques Lecercle calls folk etymology, whose aim is to dis-cover meanings through tracking the (sometimes infinitesimal) associative shifts between terms (words, places, times, events, people, jokes, texts, etc.).

While associations may be tracked homophoni-cally, graphically, metaphorically or metonymically, the key to such analyses is that all associations count; all are to be taken literally.

The litteral perspective does not therefore assume that language is a tool which humans pick up and put down at whim, nor does it suggest that it constitutes a grid through which we strain experience. The litteral perspective takes language as an organ, "a part of an organism that is typically self-contained and has a specific vital function" (*Oxford English Dictionary*). And this perspective is correct, for every language is a Tongue, that is, literally, an organ.

Like all such members, a Tongue participates in the organization of a body's experience. So just as the heart organizes blood and the kidney wastewater, a Tongue organizes the Sense, i.e., the meaning or purpose of experience.

In litteral poetics, then, language is treated as neither referential, nor as a set of impersonal and arbitrary rules, but as a (welcome) member that helps to make sense of a body—physical or psychical, individual or communal—by endowing it with reason/s through the organ-ization of its perceptions, kinships and tempers.

The aim of +|'me'S-pace is to examine such a body of organizations by making a litteral study of the English Tongue.

Chapter 1

+|'me'S-pace

Introducing space-time, which is the substance not
only of the material realm but also
of a psycholinguistic one.

In the beginning

A tongue is a connected complex even if it may sometimes slip.

We may thus commence an analysis anywhere.

For the sake of brevity, let us begin as science does, with the substance of our universe, space-time:

Space-time

But perhaps we should clarify something.

There are no singular or correct ways to understand the arrangements of a tongue.

All readings make (some) sense to some |.

(Perhaps this is the definition of a reading?)

A tongue is thus less a uni-verse, than a *multi-verse.*

|n the form|n' of

|ts Self Pr|nc|ple

LOve cOn ceived

the vV o|d se

named

FOrm e

|n the form|n' of |ts Self Pr|nc|ple LOve cOnceived the vV o|d se named FOrm e

FOrm e

named

vV o|d se the

LOve cOn ceived

|ts Self Pr|nc|ple

|n the form|n' of

So we begin again:

space-time

space-time

space-time

space-time

Space-time

Through the shifts offered by a poetic lens,
this wor(|)d may then be seen as:

time-space

time-space

time-space

time-space

time-Space

which becomes:

time'S-pace

which becomes:

t|me'S pace

which becomes:

+|'me 's pace

which becomes:

| + me = pace

| + me = pace

The multiverse breathes

me

|

me

|

me

|

me

|'m

me

|'m

me

|'m

me

me

+l'me + l'me + l'me +l'me
+l'me + l'me + l'me +l'me
+l'me + l'me + l'me +l'me
+l'me + l'me + l'me +l'me
+l'me + l'me + l'me +l'me
+l'me + l'me + l'me +l'me
+l'me + l'me + l'me +l'me
+l'me + l'me + l'me +l'me
l'me l'me l'me l'me l'me
l'me l'me l'me l'me l'me
l'me l'me l'me l'me l'me
l'me l'me l'me l'me l'me
l'me l'me l'me l'me l'me
l'me l'me l'me l'me l'me
l'me l'me l'me l'me l'me
l'me l'me l'me l'me l'me
+l'me + l'me + l'me +l'me
+l'me + l'me + l'me +l'me
+l'me + l'me + l'me +l'me
+l'me + l'me + l'me +l'me
+l'me + l'me + l'me +l'me
+l'me + l'me + l'me +l'me
+l'me + l'me + l'me +l'me
+l'me + l'me + l'me +l'me

+ I'me + I'me + I'me + I'me +
I'me + I'me + I'me + I'me
+ I'me + I'me + I'me + I'me +
I'me + I'me + I'me + I'me
+ I'me + I'me + I'me + I'me +
I'me + I'me + I'me + I'me
+ I'me + I'me + I'me + I'me +
I'me + Ivme + I'me + I'me
+ I'me + I'me + I'me + I'me +
I'me + I'me + I'me + I'me
+ I'me + I'me + I'me + I'me +
I'me + I'me + I'me + I'me
+ I'me + I'me + I'me + I'me +
I 'me + I 'me + I 'me + I 'me
+ I'me + I'me + I'me + I'me +
I 'me + I 'me + I 'me + I 'me
+ I 'me + I 'me + I 'me + I
'me + I 'me + I 'me + I 'me +
I 'me + I 'me + I 'me + I 'me
+ I + me + I + me + I + me
+ I + me + I + me + I + me
+ I + me + I + me + I + me
+ I + me + I + me + I + me
+ I + me + I + me + I + me

mmmmmmmmmmmmmmmmm
mmmmmmmm
mmmm
mm O
o o o o O | am
mmmm mm |
| am | am | am
am |
?
|m |m |m |m |m |m |m mmm
|'m |'m |'m |'m |'m |'m
|
| O | O | O | am
|'m me |'m me
| am
O
+
|'me |'me |'me + |'m me |
mm |'m mm |'m mm |'m e
+ |'m me
|'m me |'m me |
|'m me |'m me |'m me O
+
+ | me + | me + | me down
+ + | me + | me
+ | me
again
+ + | me + | me + | me down
+ + | me + + | me
+ + | me again
+
+ | me + + | me + + | me + + | me
|'m   me |'m   me |'me |'m
me me me me me me me
me me me me
me + |
| | | |
| | |
| am | am
| am
|
Ooooooooooooooooooooooh
!

+ +| me +| me +| me down

|'me |'me |'me |'me

O | O | O

| am

|'me |'me |'me

|

o

O

O

O

O

O

|'mmmm

mmmME !

the multiverse breathes

I'm

me

I'm

me

I'm

me

I'm

me

I'm

me

I'm

me

I'm

me

as the tongue shivers between

the |

+

the me

In the
verse of the English tongue
time-space |s

composed of nothing

but
the rhythmic pulse
which shivers between

the being of agent
and being _a patient:

|'m
me
|'m
me

|'m
me
|'m
me

agent and patient

_{an} |nterpiercing For-M_e.

We see why the -verse of the English tongue is multiplicitous for, as this analysis shows, even when only one language-infested being is invoked, the psycholinguistic realm is complex, not simple, being composed of both

the |

+

the me.

Taking English by the letter we discover that time-space is not only the substance of the material universe, it is also the stuff from which a *linguistic* realm is composed.

Moreover, just as the material realm can be seen as an intertwining of matter and energy, the linguistic realm is also composed of two intertwined phenomena —language and the psyche, which may be seen as different manifestations or partial aspects of a single complex phenomenon.

That is to say, just as the physical universe is constituted by a basic field of "stuff" whose convolutions account for all the material properties of being, so there is a psychic/linguistic realm composed by the positions beings may take up as theirselves, the position of the "|" and the position of the "me."

On Psycho-linguistics

Litteral poetics is thus also a form of psycho-linguistics, a method for studying psychic structure.

This is not to say that litteral poetics is the only method for analyzing psyches, or that it covers all psychic phenomena. The claim here is simply that this type of study can throw light on relations that might be less clearly illuminated by other means, which no doubt highlight their own special terrains.

On th-e-motional dynamics of linguistic t|*'me's-pace*

The method of litteral poetics not only reveals new connections between language and psyche, it also highlights the fact that a tongue is not a static entity, but is _{in} always dynamic, for the two principal components of its basic stuff, t|'me's-pace, are not just elements, but *positions:*

the position of |

\+

the position of me

po·si·tion (pə' ZI ʃ(ə)n)*
n.

1. A place occupied.
2. A bodily attitude or posture, especially a posture assumed by a patient to facilitate the performance of diagnostic, surgical, or therapeutic procedures.

**American Heritage Stedman's Medical Dictionary*

Furthermore, because this is not just the realm of the psyche, but also of language, these sites are assertions; the locations are also locutions, the positions are also *pro*-positions:

the |

+

the me

=

the position of |

+

the position of me

=

the *pro*-position of |

+

the *pro*-position of me

Taking English by the letter,
we may thus conclude that

the shimmering flow$_{er}$ of t|'me's-pace

's

th-e-motional pulse between two s|tes

the *pro*-position of $_{the}$ |
+
the *pro*-position of $_{the}$ me.

Chapter 2

+|’me ’S rh|thm

Introducing *translation*; because our tongue is not so clean as we might like, and certain non-litteral components need further interpretation.

the shimmering flow_{er} of t|'me's-pace

's

th-e-motional pulse between two pro-positions

*The second step in our examination of the English
tongue may thus commence with its pulse.*

I'm

me

I'm

me

I'm

me

I'm

me

I'm

me

| + me 'S pace

| + me = pace

But what *exactly* does "pace" mean?

Or to put the question in a more litteral manner:

what does the linguistic string "pace" tell us about psychic structure?

The answer to this question is self-evident:

"pace" is the rhythm
through which
$_a$ being pulses

between the $_{pro}$ position of its |
and the $_{pro}$ position of its me.

"Pace" is the rhythm of the psycholinguistic field.

Cleansing the tongue

At this point we realize that if litteral poetics works by making interpretations of linguistic strings, by necessity it confines us to what can be interpreted litterally. In other words, the method necessitates that all non-litteral aspects be purged from the tongue.

This can be done in two ways:

a)- either we simply ignore them, or
b)- we make a *translation* that does allow a litteral interpretation.

The latter strategy is clearly preferable, for our aim is to be as comprehensive as possible, understanding fully that all interpretations have their limits.

To understand the linguistic complex "pace" we must therefore translate it into something more litteral.

"pace" = rh|thm

Thus, just as the litterality of the poetic method allowed us to move from

space-time

to

time-space

to

+|'me'S-pace

so now we move from

+ |'me 'S pace

to the more litteral

+ |'me 'S rh|thm

or

| + me = rh|thm.

+ |'me 'S rh|+hm

|'m me

+ |'me me,

|'m the meter

t' me.

|'m the meter

| met'er,

| meet her

here.

| me +' her *here.*

because

she's o'er +*here.*

'S-pace and Ex-stasis:
Towards a definition of +|'me'S-rhythm

If the "time" portion of the psycholinguistic field is
constituted by

$$_{the}\,|\,+\,_{the}\,me$$

the two principal $_{pro}$ positions between which a being
may move,

the aspect of "space" consists in the pulse, meter,
rhythm or rate at which |t moves between them.

'S pace is thus not what is *around* the | and the me,

it is the non-static difference *between* them.

'S-pace is the ex-static difference between $_{the}$ two
"positions" of +|'me.

Or perhaps +|'me is the ecstatic difference, and 'S-
pace is composed by the two $_{pro}$ positions?

However, there is no need to define which is which,
for it is the whole complex, +|'me'S-pace, with which
we are concerned, not the components into which it
may be dissolved.

Or rather, as we have now translated this substance into
its more litteral form, what concerns us is the complex
of +|'me'S-*rhythm*, which we may now define:

+|'me'S-rhythm [tahym-es-ri*th-uh* m]*
n.

1. the ex-static difference between the $_{pro}$ position
of the | and the $_{pro}$ position of the me.

* +|'me'S-pace, bk 1, vol 2, "For Love Alone" $_{Christina\,'S\text{-}tead}$

Derivation of principal characters

As we know, the method of litteral poetics requires that we take our tongue by the letter.

Having arrived at a consistent interpretation of time-space, we are now ready to begin deriving a core group of characters.

As with whole words, the level of the letter also requires that we translate all characters into forms we can take litterally. (We should also bare in mind that, as a generality, the litteral method functions more easily if we minimize the redundancy in our formulations.)

When we translate "time" as "+|'me," we see that the characters "t" and "+" are interchangeable. We may therefore replace every "t" with a "+" and remove "t" from our +ongue.

By similar reasoning, the "|" is interchangeable with "y" and hence we can also remove the "y."

Subtracting the redundant characters from our clarified version of +|me-space:

$$\textbf{+ | ' m e ~s r h \cancel{+ + h m}}$$

leaves a core group of eight characters:

$$\textbf{+ | ' m e s r h}$$

These eight atomic characters are all a being infested with an English tongue requires to compose |ts principal sense of time-space, as it shivers between the (pro)-position of | and the (pro)-position of me.

(When you think about it, this is quite astounding.)

However, the eight are not quite enough to compose *all* categorical arrangements in the English tongue. To do this we must add two more characters; that is, we must take into account not just time-space, but also its *knots*.

Chapter 3

| / Me → | / O

Introducing the Ooooooooh of the Me.

A most important aspect of litteral poetics is its adherence to the relational view.

Atomic characters, like musical notes, only produce Sense when arranged in relational complexes, i.e., propositions.

The principal relation embodied in the compositional fragment:

$$+ \mid ' \text{ me 'S rh} \mid \text{thm}$$

is the relation of *togetherness* between

$$\text{the} \mid \ + \ \text{the me.}$$

This relation is indicated by the character:

$$"+"$$

whose qualities we explored in chapters one and two.

The third step in our examination of the English tongue looks not at the rhythmic bond of conjunction between the | and the me, but at each of these $_{pro}$positions as individuals.

The |'m-position of the me

Though _{the} | and _{the} me are both propositions, each employs a different mode of expression.

Being assertive, the proposition of the | gives the being which adopts |t a sense of agency, while that of the me imparts a sense of being-acted-upon.

In other words, while the site of the | feels like the positive position a being may take up for |tself, the site of the me is experienced as imposed.

Thus, while the site of the | may truly be considered a *pro*-position, to those whose psychic organ-ization includes an English tongue, the me is more litterally conceived as an |*m-position.*

While the *pro*-position of the | creates a sense of subjectivity, the |'*m*-position of the me imparts a sense that being is an object _{of some other.}

the pro-position of |

\+

the |'m-position of me

Sub|ect

\+

Object

_{an} |nterpiercing For-M_{e.}

We must thus reassess the structure of time-space, for now the basic components of the psycholinguistic field appear not as the | and the me, but as an | and an

O.

the Linguistic Stuff

of

+|'me'S-pace

'S

what shivers

between the $_{pro}$ position of |

and $_{|'m}$ position of me / O

| + me + | + me + | + me + | + me

+ | me | me | me | me +

| me | me | me | me

| O | O | O | O

| O | O | O | O

| O | O | O | O

| O | O | O | O

| O | O | O | O

| me | me | me | me | me
| me | me | me | me | me
| me | me | me | me | me
| O | O | O | O
| O | O | O | O
| O | O | O | O
| O | O | O | O
| O | O | O | O
| O | O | O | O

| me | me | me | me | me
| me | me | me | me | me
| me | me | me | me
| O | O | O | O
| O | O | O | O
| O | O | O | O
| O | O | O | O

| me | me | me | me | me
| me | me | me | me | me
| me | me | me | me
| O | O | O | O
| O | O | O | O
| O | O | O | O
| O | O | O | O

| me | me | me | me | me
| me | me | me | me | me
| me | me | me | me
| O | O | O | O
| O | O | O | O
| O | O | O | O
| O | O | O | O

O

O|O|O|O|O|O|O|O|O|O|O|O

O|O|O|O|O|O|O|O|O|O

OO||OO||OO||OO||

OO||OO||OO||

OOOOOOO

||||

O

thrOugh m| O

m| m| m|

LOVE   LOVE   LOVE   LOVE

Oh   Oh   Oh   Oh   Oh

                                        how

| | | |

L|VE   L|VE   L|VE

the trou of the wound on the sighed of the|'S-pace

Oh Oh Oh Oh

Oh   m|

LOVE

then comes the frOg* with |ts quest-ion.

* See "Litteral Poetics: The scUm Methodology."

From the beginning the babeling's duplicitous

the

+

the O

The | is the site of a pro-position,

the O ther of an |'m-position.

We may regard these two character-sites as the *principal principles* in our little drama.

But while the rhythmic bond that unites

the

\+

the O

constitutes the complex whole of time-space, as *individuals*, these two elements are quite different.

Our next question is, how might this "difference" be represented litterally?

Chapter 4

$_k$NO+s

Introducing the *difference* between the | and the O.

As the fourth step in our examination of the English tongue, we now focus on the relation of difference *between the | and the O.*

The method of litteral poetics attends to both linguistic characters *and* to the relations between them.

In English the relation of togetherness is marked by the character "+."

In English the relation of difference is defined as a relation of *negation* between $_{an}$ | + its O-ther.

How then is this sense of negation articulated?

In mathematics, one sign for negation is

$$-$$

Therefore we might be tempted to define the O as the "– |" or "minus-one."

However, the minus sign "–" only negates a single term: it thus represents the reverse-of-a-term, not a relationship *between terms*. Or, to put it another way, the minus sign does not represent a relation at all, for relations are triadic structures, being, as they are, composed of at least two terms plus the "difference" between them. The minus sign represents merely a simple opposition: it is a dyad, or form of secondness, not a truly triadic form of thirdness.

On the other hand, the mathematical character

$$\neq$$

does represent a form of negation that is also a relationship between terms.

The formula

$$| \neq O$$

describes the situation between the | and the O.

In English

$$| \neq O$$

or

$$\text{the } | \neq \text{the } O$$

translates litterally as

$$\text{the } \Big| - {}_k\text{N}O\text{T} = \text{the } O.$$

In other words, in English, there is

$$\text{a } {}_k\text{N}O\text{t } |\text{n the } \Big|$$

$$+$$

$$\text{this } {}_k\text{N}O\text{T } \Big|\text{n' } {}_{\text{of the}} \Big|$$

$$= {}_{\text{the}} O$$

In English, then, the site of |'m-position,
or "O,"
is articulated as

$$\text{a } {}_k\text{N}O\text{T } \Big|\text{n' } {}_{\text{of the}} \Big|.$$

This formulation of

the $_k$NOT |n' $_{of}$ the |

draws attention to the fact that the substance of

+|'me'S-pace

is not smooth, for in it there are

$_k$nOts.

$_k$N$\mathbf{O}$Ts

$$O \; = \; _{the}\Big|\text{'s} \; - \; _k\text{N}\mathbf{O}\text{T}$$

$$_{the}O \; \Big|\text{'s a } _k\text{N}\mathbf{O}\text{T}$$

$$\text{there's a } _k\text{N}\mathbf{O}\text{T} \; \Big|_{\text{n'}} \; +\Big|_{\text{'me}}\text{'}\mathbf{S}_{\text{–pace}}$$

$$\text{a } _k\text{n}\mathbf{O}\text{t} \; \Big|_{\text{n'}} \; + \; \Big|_{\text{'me}}$$

$$_k\text{n}\mathbf{O}\text{t} \; \Big|_{\text{n'X's}}$$

$$_k\text{n}\mathbf{O}+ \; \Big|_{\text{n' m}}\Big| \; \text{space.}$$

wat t |'s **+** |'Me's ₐkN O T **?**

watt |'s

X ₐ ₖN O T

watt am |
watt am |
watt am | ?
a kNot ?

watt t|'me is
watt t|'me is
watt t|'me
|'s
a kNot?

|'s
watt |'s
watt t|'me's a knOt.

watt |'s X ₐkN O T
'S

watt |'s + |'me 'S ₐpace

In English the site of the |'m position of the "O" is
articulated as

$$a\ kNOT\ |n'_{\ of\ the}\ |$$

$$a\ kNOT\ |n'_{\ of}\ +|'me'S\text{-}pace$$

or

$$a\ kNOT\ |n'_{\ of}\ +|'me'S\text{-}rh|thm.$$

Though this kNot (|n') is a component of a particular
relation of negation between terms, its psycholinguistic
affect need not be seen as wholly negative or
undesirable.

Regrettably, for beings infested with an English
tongue this is the case, for the $_k$nOt is experienced as
a wholly negative *fa|lling of $_{the}$ Sense$_{s.}$*

there's a kN**O**T |n' _{of the} |

the **O**'s the site of a fa|ll |n' _{the} |

the **O**'s a gap |n' _{the} |

a gap |n' the Sense_s

there's a kN**O**T |n' _{of the} |

the **O**'s the site where the Sense of | fa|lls

f-a|ll|n's

fa|lling, fa|lling

up + down.

the hollow e|e's

+ the grind|n' teeth

the griiiiind|n' t**ee**th

+ the sm**Ou**ther|n' v**O**|dse

the sm**Ou**ther|n' v**O**|dse

+ the be|n' in her

the be|n' |n Her

+ kN**O**T be|n' Her_e

kN**O**T be |n' Her_e

+ kN**O**T be |n' +here_.

kN**O**T|n'

Nothing

kNOT|n' here

there's nothing her_e

+ a kN**O**T thing +here_.

+ the kN**O**T a's-he, fa|lls

'n the p**O**|-sonous v**O**|dse

a' fa|lling too

the like|n'ess of her.

fa|lling to be like the like|n'ess of her,

fa|lling fa|lling

to like 't a t'all.

+ the hOllOw e|e's

+ the grind|n' t**ee**th

+ the smOUther|n' vO|ds_e

+ the kNOT |n the e|e,

the kNOT|n' the |

that a-vO|ds |+ to see

the vO|ds_e 'n the s|ght

of the kNot|n'

+ |'me'**S**-pace.

+ kNOT be |n' here

+ kNOT be |n' +here

kNOT be|n' |n the e|e

+ kNOT bein' |n the h|men,

kNOT be|n' Her_d

+ kNOT be|n' s**ee**n.

+ the kNOT-a's-he, fa|lls

'n the pO|-sonous vO|ds_e

a' fa|lling to be

the like|n'ess of her,

fa|lling fa|lling to be like her

fa|lling fa|lling

the hOllOw |s,

the hOllOw |s,

+ the grind|n' to be

+he kNOT in the e|e.

of ₖNO***T*** |n t|me's space,

the kNO***T***ing time

NO***thing*** time

ₖNO***T*** |n +|'me' S-pace .

+ the kNO***T***-a's-he, fa|lls

'n the p**O**|-sonous v**O**|dse

a' fa|lling to be

the like|n'ess of her,

fa|lling fa|lling to be like her

fa|lling fa|lling

the h**O**ll**O**w |s,

the h**O**ll**O**w |s,

+ the grind|n' to be

+he kN**O**T in the e|e.

of ₖN**O**T |n t|me's space,

the kNO***T***ing time

N**O**thing time

ₖN**O**T |n +|'me' S-pace .

Chapter 5

Principal Characters

Taking account of both

$$+|\text{' me'S-pace}$$

and its

$$_k\text{nOt-}|\text{n's}$$

we derive an atomic alphabet of 10 principle-characters:

	'	s	n	O	+	h	e	m	r
1	2	3	4	5	6	7	8	9	10

Having recognized the $_k nOt$-|n's of+|'me'S-rh|thm, as the fifth step in our examination, we conclude the roll call of characters by introducing the final two principals of our set.

The method of litteral poetics attends to both the relations between linguistic characters, and to the characters-in-themselves.

In chapter 1 we focused on the relation of togetherness between the | and the me.

In chapter 2 we derived a group of eight principals:

+ | ' m e s r h

In chapter 3 we reassessed the "me," leading to the addition of an "O" on our list.

We now have nine characters in our core group.

+ | ' m e s r h O

However, by introducing the "O," we also surreptitiously brought in another character, namely the "n."

Thus, we have now derived an atomic alphabet of 10 principal characters:

| ' s n O + h e m r
1 2 3 4 5 6 7 8 9 10

and can finally construct

"A Familyar Drama"

How to _{de} Compose a Body:
A Corpus in 3 Acts

Prelude

> At the heart of a would
> in the eye of a tongue
> lies the stuff-|n'-|tself
> made up by the |'s
> whose relations compose
> every body of word(er)s.

At the heart of Language, every language, lies a subjectless combinatoric, the impersonal stuff-in-|tself of the characters whose relations compose each body in words.

Improvisatory Remarks

The drama of this corpus is neither fixed nor complete, offering ever new arrangements to the e|e, ear, body and mind. It is thus necessarily improvisatory, not scripted. The following are suggestions for rehearsal only. Any actual drama consists in the arrangements parties make for themselves.

Setting

Every evening, just about lightening up time………..

Dramatis Personae

A familyar group, comprised of 10 principles:-

$$|\ '\ s\ n\ O\ +\ h\ e\ m\ r$$
1 2 3   4   5   6   7 8   9 10

Like the notes on a scale, or the points in a plane, these characters—or linguistic atoms—are bound by relations which are what they are whatever we think. Because of these connections, the principals may compose themselves into the molecular or chord-like arrangements that we call Words.

Act 1: On Word$_{er}$s

Consists of the principles, the ten familyar characters:

|'s n O + h e m r

exploring their relations by arranging themselves in a variety of word-like affairs. Examples of such arrangements may include, but are not limited to, the following:-

|	e|e	One	sOn
me	|'m	m|	m|ne
he	she	h|m	her
+he|	+hem	+he|r	+he|rs
h|s	hers	+he	+h|s
|+	+	|n	+o
here	+here	+hen	|s
he's	she's	one's	+he|'s
some	men	o+her	o+hers
o+her's	mo+her	mo+hers	mo+her's
'S-mO+her	S-mO+her's	S-mO+her|n'	h|men
h|mn	's+Or|	h|s+Or|	+|'me
nO	nO+	nOne	nO+h|n'
'S-ense	nOn'S-ense	|n'S-ense	es'S-ense
ense	sen+	resen+	re-'S-ense

And just as words can be composed from the affairs of characters, so they themselves may be arranged into the higher order complexes known as Propositions.

Act 2: Indecent Proposals

Consists of the principles composing their affairs into familyar structures through meaningful propositions. For example:-

+he |	|s	+he sOn
+he	|'s	+h$_e$|'S-One
|	|s	nO+ +he O+her
he	|s	nO+ her
+he	|'s	nO+ +hemO+hers
+h$_e$|'S-One	's	nO+ +hemO+hers
+ |'m Me	|s	+|'me
+|'me	|'s	+h|s'S+Or|
+h$_e$|'SONe	's	+h$_e$|s'S+Or|
+h$_e$|s'S+Or|	of	+he $_e$|$_e$ which $_+$he's in all ways $_{be}$coming through the h|MeN of +hemO+her's

Improvisatory Remarks

Propositions may in their turn be composed into the even more complex arrangements known as Inferences, but the exploration of these must await further occasion.

What is more, despite the infinite arrangements players make for themselves from the initial principles of this drama, it is clear that the entire English Corpus may not be constituted from these ten alone. New characters must be added if we are to compose it fully. For example, adding the character "a" allows our body to develop through the following complexifications:-

an   an | an | an |-|

he's   no+   an |-| he's no+ |, he's +he sone

he's   a no+ a her   she's ano+her

+hem O+hers are man | +he mo+her's ano+her

+he |'s-One's nO+   +he-m-an |-o+her's

The ten principles of this script should not then be seen as either a definitive list or a necessary core. The set is arbitrary, and the point is not to assert some fundamental thesis, but to see what happens when this group is allowed to work through the flow_{ering} of its relations undisturbed.

The surprise of this event is the range of categories which may be elicited from the stream. Thus, where the performance suggested above focuses on Time, Quantity, Gender and Generation, other plays might highlight Space, Quality, Possession and Relation, to mention only Space, Quality, Possession and Relation, and Time, Quantity, Gender and Generation. Even more surprising is these categories' flexibility, as many easily morph into others. Thus +|me becomes + |'Me, a category which seemingly combines subjection with objection, and possession with action. While the unquantifiable O+her quickly sublimates into the fluid, flowing multiplicity of the All of +he-M-O+hers.

From this perspective, the aim of each drama is not to propose an "objective" thesis, but to constitute a particular categorical breakdown from the play of the given characters, charting their vicissitudes as they compose themselves into ever more complex arrangements. For example:-

_{the} |'s nO+ here nO+ me nOr +here

nO +|'me nOr 'S-ense +O me Or +hem

_{for} he's nO+ 's he's _anO+ he's _anO+her_e

he's +h_e|'S-On_e +O +heMO+her_e's ?

Having explored a portion of this initial field, players may wish to take on other character_{istic}s.

The drama ends when either the combinations of characters are exhausted—an unlikely event—or the players just can't keep it up anymore. At this point The End is declared.

Remarks Prepatory to an Ending

While the above-mentioned characters are not actually persons, Language is something that beings may assume.

Despite appearances, this assumption is not inevitable. However, its rejection has consequences, for by it a being refuses its own articulate _{relat}ions.

On the other hand, if the assumption is made, a radical transformation occurs, as the affairs of a language shift from the impersonal to the personal mode, when beings adopt them as the Characters-in-Themselves.

However, these characters are not adopted singly but *en masse*, in complex propositions whose unfolding, and ever-branching, inferences constitute the passages through which each speaking e|e articulates |tself in this world.

Act 3: Finale: An Anti-Obituary, or The Assumption

The final act is non-improvisatory, and consists of a chorus invoked by all principles, calling upon the audience to give them life.

Chorus: "Assume a position now!"

"Assume a *pro*-position NOW!"

Chapters 1 through 4 explored the psycholinguistics of a single subject. This lead us to focus on the subject's sense of Object-ifica-tion to the |'m-position of a $_k$nOt.

Examining this $_k$nOt in turn enabled us to include enough characters that we have now moved from the relations internal to subjects, to the relations that come between them: we have shifted from a focus on individual psyches infested by an English tongue to the study of *whole families* of concepts.

Chapter 6

Familyar Categories

Introducing those relations in the familyar drama of
English which have a recurring structure of
$_k$nOts.

Having settled on a core group of characters, in the sixth step of our examination we derive a set of core relations, or "categories."

If, as we have seen,
there is

a

$_k$NOT
|n'

of the +|'me'S-pace

of each |ndividual psyche,

|n

the +|'me'S-pace

of a complex
composed by a network of relations
between different individuals

there are *many* such tangles.

What we call "the family"
is just such a complex.

The Corpus in Chapter 5 shows that there are many propositional complexes structured around ₖnOts.

the |'s not here, not me nor there

no t|me nor sense to me or them,

for he's not she's a not he, another

he's the|'-s-one to the-m-others.

|'s nOt me

the |'s 'nOther

m|ne's nOt the|rs

here |s nOt there

he |s nOt her

the |'s nOt them

the |'Sone's nOt the-m-Others

As we see, these propositions constitute some of the most important *categories* in the English Tongue.

+ he |'s nO+ me

> Time - (In-tension-Will)

here |s nO+ +here

> Space - (Ex-tension-Stasis)

+he |'s nO+ +hem

> Quantity - (Number)

he |s nO+ her

> Quality - (Gender)

+he |'s 'nO+her

> Action - (Subjection)

m|ne's nO+ +he|rs

> Passivity - (Objection)

+he |'Son$_e$'s nO+ +he-mO+hers

> Relation - (Generation)

In chapter 4 we saw that the $_k nOt_{|n}$'s $_{of}$ $_{the}$ | could be described by the formula:

$$| \neq O$$

However, in the propositions of the Corpus the structure of the $_k nOt$ is not

$$|\text{-}_k nOt = O$$

but rather

the | 's nO+ the O

| 's nO+ O

$$| = nO+ O$$

that is

$$| = - O$$

the | = the minus O.

$$| = - \mathbf{O}$$

the | = the minus O

even if, *by convention* the "|" is ₍usually₎ considered the *positive* term, and the "O" the *negative,*

that is, even if we often define the relation in reverse as

the O = the minus |

$$\mathbf{O} = - |$$

But this is the nature of dyadic forms, that the two reciprocally define each other.

Such a mutually defining form of negation between two terms does *not*, as has been said, constitute a relation proper, but rather a case of simple opposition.

From the Corpus, we see that many of the most commonly used categories of the English tongue are structured around this non-relational form of opposition.

+ he |'s nO+ me

> Time - (In-tension-Will)

here |s nO+ +here

> Space - (Ex-tension-Stasis)

+he |'s nO+ +hem

> Quantity - (Number)

he |s nO+ her

> Quality - (Gender)

+he |'s 'nO+her

> Action - (Subjection)

m|ne's nO+ +he|rs

> Passivity - (Objection)

+he |'Son$_e$'s nO+ +he-mO+hers

> Relation - (Generation)

These "categories" present themselves as categories-of-relations.

In this English infested body of propositions, even our most familyar category

$$+ |\text{'me}$$

is composed around the formula of opposition

$$| = - O$$

$$| = \text{not-O.}$$

$$|\text{'s not-O}$$

$$_{\text{the}} |\text{'s not }_{\text{the}} O$$

$$+ \text{he } |\text{'s nO+ me}$$

in which the O is seen as merely the negation of the |.

In chapter 4 we encountered a version of the English tongue in which

_{the} O

was understood as

a _kNOT $|$n' _{of the} $|$

that is

a _kNOT $|$n' _{of} +$|$'me'S-pace

or

a _kNOT $|$n' _{of} +$|$'me'S-rh$|$thm.

In this formulation the relation of difference between the $|$ and the O was conceived around the structure

$$|\neq O.$$

Through the Corpus we now see that in the current state of $|$ts self-conception, the English tongue does *not* view difference in this way. In fact, English does not currently conceive of the form of negation that comes between the $|$ and the O as a relation at all, but rather as the *negation of all relations*......

$|$'s not-O

_{the} $|$'s not _{the} O

+ he $|$'s nO+ me

+ he $|$'s no + $|$' me

no + $|$' me at all......

|n-WrUptur|n' th|'Space

1. wrap+|n' +h|'space be+ween   wrapped in the space between
    her + | 'me   her time
    's he 's no + he 's   she's not he's
    a no + he a no + her.   a not-he a not-her.

2. wrap+|n' +h|'space be+ween   wrappin' this pace between
    heure + | 'me   her time
    's he 's no + he 's   she's not he's
    an o + he no + her.   an 0 the 'n0ther.

3. wrap+|n' +h|'space be+ween   wrapt in the space between
    her + | 'me   her and one me-
    's he 's no + me 's   she's not me's
    no + her e no + her e.   not here no' there.

4. wrup+|n' th|'space be+ween   wruptin' the space between
    her + | 'me   her and I-me
    's he 's no + me   she's not me
    + | 'me no + her e.   and I'm not here.

5. |n wrup+|n' th|'space which |'S   in wrupturin' this pace which IS
    heure + | 'me   hour time
    's he 's no + more   she's not me
    + | 'me no |.   and I'm no-one.

6. |n wrup+|n' th|'space which |'S   in wrupturin' the space which I's
    hour + | 'me   our time
    's he 's no + here   she's not here
    + | 'me no + more   and I'm no more.

               ...... + |'me no more.

     Noooooooooooooooooooooooooooooooooooooooooo!

                    NO +|'ME
                NO +|'ME, NO +|'ME
            NO +|'ME, NO +|'ME, NO +|'ME
                NO +|'ME, NO +|'ME.
                    NO + |'ME
                      O + |
                       O |
                        ?

In these corporeal propositions,

not only is

the ₖNOT |n' of the |

conceived as ₐ fa|lling,

|t is experienced as a

smOUther|n'

which a-vO|ds

the | to see

anything at all.

In this truly negative conception

the ₖNOT |n' of

+|'me' S-pace

is conceived not just as

a site

that obliterates Sense

(including the senses

of time and space themselves)

|t is a site that

Obliterates

relations altogether.

In other words, in those currently infested with an English tongue, the O is not seen as a $_{pro}$ position because |t is conceived as that which *negates $_{pro}$ positionality altogether.*

This is why |t is experienced as such an |'m-position.

Here, the | does not just find

the NOT

difficult to bear,

|t conceives of it as

the complete vO|ding

or

Obliteration $_{of}$ |tself.

||
||| |||
me me me me
he he he he he he
+he +he +he +he +he
no+ he no+ he no +he no + he no + he

+ no + Me no + Me + Me

ˌno +│'ME ˌno +│'ME ˌno +│'ME

~│'me, ~│'me, ~│'me, ~│'me
~│'me, ~│'me, ~│'me, ~│'me
~│'me, ~│'me, ~│'me, ~│'me
~│'me, ~│'me, ~│'me, ~│'me
~│'me, ~│'me, ~│'me, ~│'me
~│'me, ~│'me, ~│'me, ~│'me

~│'me, ~│'me, ~│'me, ~│'me
~│'me, ~│'me, ~│'me, ~│'me
~│'me, ~│'me, ~│'me, ~│'me
~│'me, ~│'me, ~│'me, ~│'me
~│'me, ~│'me, ~│'me, ~│'me
~│'me, ~│'me, ~│'me, ~│'me

~│'me, ~│'me, ~│'me, ~│'me
~│'me, ~│'me, ~│'me, ~│'me
~│'me, ~│'me, ~│'me, ~│'me
~│'me, ~│'me, ~│'me, ~│'me
~│'me, ~│'me, ~│'me, ~│'me
~│'me, ~│'me, ~│'me, ~│'me

ₖno +│'ME ₖno +│'ME ₖno +│'ME
+ no + Me no + Me + Me
no+ he no+ he no +he no + he no + he
no+ No+ No+ no+
+he +he +he +he +he
he he he he he
me me
||||
||
Ooooooohhhhh!!

$$+ \; he \; \big|\text{'s no} + \big|\text{'} me$$

But it is not just the category of +|'me that suffers this diminishment.

All of the most familyar categories are conceived as the form | = – O, in which the Other pole is seen as merely |'s negation. In the constitution of the current English tongue,

|'s nO+ me

+he |'s 'nO+her

m|ne's nO+ +he|rs

here |s nOt there

he |s nOt her

+he |'s nO+ +hem

+he |'Sone's nO+ +he-m-O+hers

This diminishment might not matter so much were it not for its effect on the most family-ar classification, that strange category which, in English, combines both gender and generation, the category of Relation itself: the category that in current English is composed of the *complete opposition* between

$$+he|\text{'Son}_e$$

$$+$$

$$+he\text{-}mO\text{+}hers$$

Chapter 7

+he |'Son_e's and +he-M-o+her's _a kNot

The final verse, in which is addressed
the issue of family *positions*.

The seventh step in our process looks at the effects of the form | = not-O   on the relations within the nuclear family.

Duplicity and the Familyar

From chapter 3 we recall that:

from the beginning the babeling's duplicitous

What matters however is not the duplicity itself, but
that the | is explicitly equated with the position of
the Son, and the O with the position of the-Mother's
being. When the-m-Others are further conceived as
merely the negation of the|'Sone's being, we are in
real trouble.

From the beginning the babeling's duplicity

split by the vO|ds$_e$ between watt's

Her$_e$ + $_a$ $_k$Not

reinin' reinin' down from the sk$_e$|$_e$s

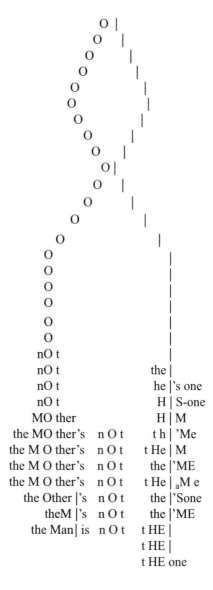

In contemporary bodies infested by English, the son defines itself in opposition to the all of the-m-Others.

The |'Sone focuses exclusively on the relation of negative difference between |tself + them-O-thers, forgetting completely the relation of togetherness.

For this reason, when any _{of them} others do try to relate to the|'Son_e in a together|n' way, |t feels overwhelmed, that is S-mothered.....

the | is mothered

| is mothered

| 's mothered

| ' s-mothered

| ' smothered

the |'S-one

'S-mothered

'S-mothered

In this way the-M-Other is defined as a smother|n'.

The current self-conception of the English tongue is pervaded by the forgetting of the relationship of togetherness represented in the crystal of

$$+|'Me$$

and by an overvalorization of the relationship of negative difference, schematized by the formula

$$| = - O$$

or

$$| = \text{not } O$$

This forgetting, and this overvalorization have enormous consequences for the psycho-social organization of those bodies infested with an English tongue.

The two most important of these include:

a) the complete reduction of possible $_{pro}$ positions within the familiar complex

b) the relation of $|$'sone to the $vO|dse$.

Reduction of Possible Propositions to
the-m-others + the |'Sone

In bodies infested by English, the categories of gender
and generation are now so entangled, and so perverted
by the non-relational $_k$NOT, that only two familyar $_{pro}$
positions are currently articulable, that of

+he-mO+her's (being)

and that of

+he|'Son$_e$'s.

In English, no other familyar $_{pro}$ positions may currently
be decried outloud.

In other words, in English, the Son defines |tself by
distinguishing |tself as a being *unique* from $_{the}$ all of
the-m-Others.

This shows that the ideology of opposition is not only
deeply embedded in English, but that in a body (social
or individual) infested by English, the positions of
the *father* and *daughter* have no possibility of being
instantiated, for there are no pro-positions through
which they might be $_{pro}$ posed

If, then, we wish to overcome this oppositional
and reductive binarism in our social relations, we
must try to find a way to express $_{these}$ more complex
arrangements in our psycholinguistic multiverse.

One aim of

"For Love Alone"
Christina 'S-tead

is to begin doing just that.

The Mother, the| 'Sone, and the vO|dse

Secondly, in English, the-m-Other's conceived as a pure vO|d$_{se}$

a vO|dse that 'S$_a$mOther|n'.

the $_e|_e$'S-on$_e$'s in the light

+

the vO|dce in the density.

WhOrd-spOke-N' fraG-meants ?

'''
                's pAce NO + |'me ?
                's pAke NO + |'me ?
                's pOke NO + |'me ?
who   's pAke NO + |'me ?
who   's pOke NO + e|e'me ?
who   's pAce NO + e|e'me ?
'''

'smouther|n' vO|dce
's mOuther |n' vO|dce ?
| 's mOUther |n' vO|dce ?
| 's mOuthere |n' the vO|dce ?
| 's mOUth there |n' the vO|dce ?
| 's me Outhere |n' the vO|dce ?
e|e's me Outthere |n' the vO|dce ?
e|e'sme Out-there |n' the vO|dce ?
+ e|e'sme Out-there |n' the vO|dce ?
+ e|e' Me Out-there |n' the vO|dce ?

's Mouther|n' vO|dce ?

th|'smOther |n' vO|dce
's mOther |n' wO|ds.

|+'s mOther |n' vO|dce ?
or 's she in the wO|ds ?

where 's me mOther
|n th|'smother|n' vvO|ds ?

                ******
th|'smOUther |n' vO|dce
's mOUther |n' wOv|ds.

|+'s mOUther |n' vO|dce ?
or 's |+ in the wO|ds ?

where 's me mOUth
|n th|'smOUther|n' vvO|ds ?

| 's |+ here |n' the vO|ce
or there |n' the vO|dse ?
here |n' the wO|ds
out there |n' the vO|d.
here |n' the wO|ds

Here, not only is

the ₋ₖN**O**Ts │n' of the │'sonₑ

conceived as a fa│lling,

│t is also experienced as a

sm**Ou**ther│n'

which a-v**O**│ds the │ to see.

Here,

the ₖN**O**Ts │n' of the │'sonₑ

that is,

the N**O**T │n of +│'me' S-pace,

is conceived as

a site

that obliterates both Sense and senses,

including the senses

of time + space themselves.

smother|n' vo|dse

'tween her + |' me is a pownder|n' vo|dce
a 'smother|n', 'smOther|n' 'smOuther|n' flow_{er}.

the 'smoutherin', 'smother|n', 'smOther|n' e|e's
find|n', found|n', founder|n' sounds
scatter|n' scatter|n'
the patterns of e|e
forME'd by the kNOts
of the poisonous vO|dce.

the pownder|n' pownder|n' pownder|n' vo|dce
of kNOt be|n' here and kNOt be|n' there.

_knO+ be|n' the|-SON_g
nOr be|n' the H|Me_N
_knO+ be|n' me
+
_knO+ be|n' the-M_{en}.

+he |'Sone's nO+ +heM$_{en|}$O+hers

+h$_e$|'Son$_g$'s nO+ +he h|m$_e$n

+he |$_s$ SOn$_g$'s $_e$ |$_e$ 'S n O+

+he M$_{en|}$ O+ $_{her's}$ h |$_{men}$

$_{+he}|_s$ SOn$_g$'s$_e|_e$ 'S n O+$_{+he}$M$_{en|}$

O+$_{her's}$ flOw$_{er}$|n' v VO|$_d$s$_e$

$_k$nO+ be|n' the|-SON$_g$
nOr be|n' the H|Me$_N$
$_k$nO+ be|n' me
+
$_k$nO+ be|n' the-M$_{en}$.

Thus concludes our story,

which has taken us from

the gentle pulsing of +|'me'S-pace

between

the poles of the individual psyche,

to

the letters of a script,

the categories of a vocabulary,

and the propositions of a family,

finally landing us in

a linguistic ditch where

neither fathers nor daughters,

men nor women

can articulate themselves;

for all that can be uttered

is the sound of

the _LOnly |

's-creaming |tself

in a vO|_dse

Conclusion

$_k$NO+s Beyond NOts

Having examined the problem, below are some notes towards the beginning of a resolution.

The fact that oppositional relations are the defining feature of current English-language categories does not prove that opposition is essential to the structuring of language *per se*. Not only can we make other categorical propositions from the ten atomic characters without using the "| = not-O" superstructure, (try it and see), but we can obtain exactly the same basic categories, only charging them with a different intent-sity, if we $_{in}$form them with *a double knot*, rather than a single one. The overall structure of the double-knot is:

$$| = \text{not-not-O}$$

or

$$|\text{'s not-not-O}$$

Applying this new formula gives the new set of propositions:

|'s nO+ nO+-+hem = Quantity - (Number)

he |s 'nO+ nO+-her = Quality - (Gender)

|'s nO+ nO+-me = Time - (In-tension-Will)

here |s nO+ nO+-+here = Space - (Ex-tension-Stasis)

+he |'s nO+-'nO+her = Action - (Subjection)

m|ne's nO+ nO+-+he|rs = Passivity - (Objection)

+he|'Sone's nO+ nO+-+he-mO+hers =
Relation - (Generation)

Though these new complexes still make the same basic categories, the relationship between the poles is no longer oppositional. The question is now, how we make practical sense of these new versions of our categories? In particular, how can we make sense of the new version of the category of genderation?

In classical logic, the double negation "not-not" either returns the speaker to her original $_{pro}$position or produces a paradox. However, some non-classical logics employ forms of negation that, when reiterated, do not terminate in either of these options but rather lead to wholly new realms. We are even familiar with this phenomenon in everyday language. For instance, take the word "dressed;" one of its negations is "not-dressed." But it also has another, "undressed." The difference between these two is nicely made in visual art as the distinction between the naked and the nude. Now ask yourself: if it is not to be re-clothed, what is it to be not-un-dressed? By the same $_{non\text{-}classical}$ logic, if not-| is the Other, and un-| is the-m-others, what is $_{the}$ not-un-|? What is the Other to the-m-Others?

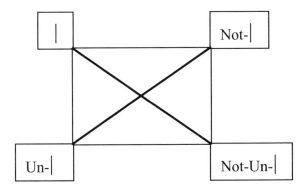

According to some forms of contemporary analysis, this is a nonsensical question, because, they declare, "there is no other of the Other." However, our question is slightly different, it being, not "what is the other of The Other," but "what is the other of the-M-Others?" Though there is only a single letter's difference here, it makes all the difference, for now both forms of negation/difference are acknowledged—the difference between the | and the O, and the difference between the | and the-M-any-|s—and each of these is acknowledged as being different from the other. The question is, how are we to effectively make practical sense of this difference between differences? How are we to make lived social sense of

+he|'Sone

which defines |tself as:

the nO+ nO+ of +he-mO+hers?

This question is the principal object of

"For Love Alone"

Christina 'S-tead.

It is a question of gender and generation, of how we can have both men and women, and fathers and daughters, not just the s-Ones who define themselves as unique, and set themselves apart from everyone else, whom they dismissively conceive as just the-M-any-Others.

Afterword

+|*'Me'S-pace (doc. 001b)* is an introduction to a wider poetic examination of English, entitled

> *"For Love Alone"*
> *Christina'S-tead*

The project has two main aspects, presented respectively in volumes 1 and 2. The first, to be published second, concerns the diachronic aspect which explores the conception of $_{its\ own}$ history embodied in English. The second concerns the synchronic aspect, that is, how this tongue manifests its structure now.

+|*'Me'S-pace (doc. 001b)* is book 1 of the second, synchronic volume, providing an introduction to both litteral poetics—the society's method—and some of the most familyar of current English categories.

The reader should remember that this is an ongoing project in which more attention should be paid to the method than to the conclusions currently presented, these having been superceded upon the date of publication.

Outline of Overall Project

> *"For Love Alone"*
> *Christina'S-tead*

Volume 1 : +H|'Story

> Book 1 - The Ur-Time : Genesis
> Book 2 - Heaven : Finnegans Wa$_n$ke
> Book 3 - Hell : Watt ?
> Book 4 - The Myth of the VO|ds$_e$

Volume 2 : M|th'Story   or   hO-ur'Story

> Book 1 - +|'me 'S-pace
> Book 2 - m| 'S|ster + e|e
> Book 3 - +he-M-O-+her's +he vO|dce
> Book 4 - Urth Po-$_{for}$e-Me-s

Acknowledgements

This book would not have been possible without the generous gift of ideas from many others. I would especially like to thank:

Francis Mulhern, Marie-Laure Davenport, Vincent Dachy, Bridget MacDonald, Matthew Timmons, Janet Sarbanes, Matias Viegener, and my beloved mentor, Bernard Burgoyne.

Heart felt gratitude is also owed to my publishers Vanessa Place (for dying to publish this work) and Teresa Carmody without whose patience and consummate editing skills even _{the} | could not read it, and to my dear friend Dodie Bellamy for her generous introduction.

Lastly _{the} | would like to thank all those who helped make me the person she ought to be, including my siblings, my friends, Cameron Allan +

my mother Barbara and sister Margaret.

$$(p+r)^n$$

The society for cUm|n' linguistics, scUm, is dedicated to the exploration and appreciation of the L|f,e in the English Tongue. Simultaneously laboratory and funhouse, scUm provides immersive experience in L|f,eized English through carefully staged experiments in its worders.

Lisa Darms has an MFA in photography from the University of Washington, and is currently studying History and Archival Management at New York University. She is a regular artistic collaborator with the band Growing, creating the videos 'Peace Offering" in 2006, and "Always, Already" —a 30-minute video for a live performance at APEX Art in New York—in 2005.

Dodie Bellamy is the author of *Feminine Hijinx* (Hanuman, 1990)*; Cunt Ups* (Tender Buttons, 2002); *Fat Chance* (Normados, 2004); *Pink Steam (*Suspect Thoughts, 2004); *Academonia* (Krupskaya Books, 2007); and co-author of *The Letters of Mina Harker and Sam D'Allesandra* (Talisman House, 1995).

LES FIGUES PRESS

PO Box 35628

Los Angeles, CA 90035

www.lesfigues.com